Control Your Credit Destiny

*Your Personal Credit and Wealth Building
Advisor & Creator of your Blueprint to Credit
and Financial Success*

John A. Little

authorHOUSE®

AuthorHouse™
1663 Liberty Drive, Suite 200
Bloomington, IN 47403
www.authorhouse.com
Phone: 1-800-839-8640

First published by AuthorHouse 7/26/2007

ISBN: 978-1-4343-2658-4 (sc)

Printed in the United States of America
Bloomington, Indiana

This book is printed on acid-free paper.

Dedication

I dedicate this book to my parents Aldrich and Jane Little. You have always supported me in all of my endeavors and everything that I have set out to do. Thank you for giving me the encouragement to always try new things, instilling the fearlessness for trying things I've never thought feasible and for the spiritual and moral grounding to never revel too much in the joys nor wallow in the sorrows of life.

Also I dedicate this book to my late sister Cynthia Harmon. You are with me every day and I know you would be so excited and proud that I am writing this book. I will always carry your memory and unbelievably positive spirit with me and watch your light shine through Dominique and Morgan.

Table of Contents

Acknowledgements

I want to acknowledge . . . .

*Cynthia May for your encouragement, your supportive spirit, your patience, your friendship and love throughout the writing process.

*Derrick Whitmore, Stephen Williams, Andre Walker and Chris Anglin for your friendship, your constant encouragement, your motivation and for all of our great discussions that always stimulate new thoughts and ideas. We'll make onto Oprah before we're done!!

*Dante Mc Dowell for your insight, your help, your information and your support as a friend and business partner. We have come a long way together and will continue to grow our respective businesses and achieve our goals.

*Kim Nelson for giving me the opportunity to grow and learn quickly in the mortgage business which ultimately led to me getting the inspiration and information for writing this book.

*Shane Darrisaw for seeing the potential in me and pushing me to do things I didn't even know were possible. You've taught and mentored me for the past couple of years and I look forward to learning more from you as a life long friend.

*Tim Grant, Dr. Dennis Felder, Vera Stepp and Dr. Fred Eady from Winston Salem State University for instilling in me the knowledge that I could achieve anything I wanted to, endless support and encouragement and the passion for public speaking that I will carry into the next stages of my career and life.

And of course, Ann McIndoo, my Author's Coach, who got this book out of my head and into your hands.

Introduction

This book is written as a result of my desire to help YOU achieve your financial destiny.

This book is written for anyone who wants to have a positive impact on their finances and their families.

I am writing this book because I have seen too many potential millionaires walk out of my office with nothing but disappointment and frustration because their credit precluded them from making a positive financial step for themselves or their families. If I had a dollar for everyone that I've educated on credit that said, "They really should teach this in high school" I would be a rich man. I want to share with you what I have learned so you can realize your financial destiny.

This book will help you, in a variety of ways, learn the secrets of the credit scoring formulas, how good credit is as easy as 3-2-1 and how you can begin to build wealth through homeownership without spending one penny. By the time you are done with this book you will be armed with the knowledge to go out and begin shaping your finances the way you always wanted them to be.

To your financial success!!

John A. Little

Chapter 1:

Credit and Finances Today

When I first started writing this book I didn't start out to write a horror story, but these numbers just might scare the pants off you.

- By the end of 2006, Americans had accumulated $2.4 TRILLION in consumer debt.
- In America, the median household income increased 7% from 2002 to 2006. However, in that same time period, personal consumer debt increased 21% — three times the rate of income.
- Personal bankruptcy filings in 2005 increased 66% from the year 2000.
- Debt with finance companies, which are your store credit cards, are high-risk unsecured personal loans, which as we will discuss in future chapters are credit killers, increased 75% from 2002 to 2006.
- Average credit cards rates are 13.21%. To understand what that means, visualize being at the bottom of a half-filled swimming pool trying to swim your way to the top and someone is standing at the top of that pool with a fire hose on full blast. That's what it's like when you make only your minimum monthly payments on high-interest credit cards. You eventually may get to the top, but it won't be

without taking in a whole lot of water—and you may just drown.

- A 2007 survey by Sallie Mae, the federal agency that lends and services most student loans in America, indicated that more than 50% of graduating college students had <u>more than $5,000</u> in revolving credit card debt.
- The same study showed that 33% of graduating college students had <u>$10,000 or more</u> in revolving credit card debt. Those numbers do not include <u>one penny</u> of student loan debt.

For many of us, our financial foundation was set at birth. We are thrust into the financial situation of our parents, which usually carries on into our young adulthood. It's something I like to call *silver spoon, rusty spoon,* and *just a spoon.*

As of 2005, 15% of U. S. households earn $100,000 or more. This comprises the highest income class in American society. A large percentage of this group are homeowners. Those are the people who were born with a *silver spoon.* This is a term that has been used for years to demonstrate that they were born into a life of privilege and they either may not have the same need to utilize credit to help build wealth or just maybe, they've already mastered the system and are putting a lot of principles you'll read about in this book into practice.

According to 2005 U. S. Census Bureau stats, 43% of U. S. households over 123 million are at 80% or less of the national median income of $46,326. In the housing industry that is what is considered low to moderate income. This *"rusty spoon"* crowd may have less fiscal education and more financial obstacles to overcome. However, with the loan programs and education that are available today in conjunction with the resources that are available at the city, county, state, and federal levels, this segment has the greatest opportunity to attain wealth through home ownership.

Over 155 million people — or 54% of the U.S. population — are what comprise the *"just a spoon"* crowd. *Just a spoon* is what you would typically consider the middle class. Currently, 60% of the *just a spoon* crowd are home owners. However, this segment usually has the most debt — either student loans or consumer debt — and worse credit than either of the other segments. Starting home ownership at a very young age is the key for this segment of the population. That is one thing that you will see throughout the book that home ownership is the number one key to wealth in the U.S. Over 80% of the millionaires in the US are first generation millionaires. They've achieved this through business, industry, the lottery and for a large number of people, homeownership. David Bach has a book series titled "Automatic Millionaire" which focuses a large amount of attention on homeownership. The core concept, purchasing real estate, letting it appreciate, selling for a large profit and moving onto the next deal. When done right, it's one of the best money making vehicles available to every American. Here's the kicker (you don't even need one cent to get started.)

The very first step in shaping your credit destiny is to do an honest assessment of your current and credit financial situation. The prevailing notion is that credit scores are based on past performance as an indication of future behavior. What your credit score does is it gives those who are going to extend credit to you an idea of what they can expect when it comes to repaying the debt. As we'll discuss in a future chapter, your credit score and credit history tell your creditors who you were but not necessarily who you are. Take a few minutes to actually review your credit report. Do an honest assessment of where you are. If your credit is poor, then say it's poor, but commit to making the improvements to put yourself in a better financial situation. Don't live in the past—live in the present and plan for the future.

Reality is a fluid concept when it comes to a credit score. Your credit score changes every month, and you and you alone have the ability to affect positive change. I personally have seen my own credit score improve 70 points in only six months. Take ownership of the things on your credit report—good, bad, right, or wrong. Take the steps to make sure that your credit report reflects an accurate indication of who you are today. It's not always easy—you may have to dig out of a hole. But I can guarantee you this—once you get your credit report in good standing, it's always rewarding.

In corporate America we have an acronym-BHAG which means "Big Hairy Audacious Goal". A BHAG is something that when you say it out loud and when you write it on paper, it looks completely unattainable but sets your long term vision. The key with a BHAG—or any other goal that you set—is that you have to believe it, you have to live it and you have to do everything in your power to achieve it. As you'll see throughout this book, goal setting is an important step in achieving your financial goals and securing your financial freedom.

Another theme that you'll see throughout this book is

homeownership is the number one key to wealth in America. You're not going to find the magic lottery numbers in this book. However, I will give you exactly what you need to know to start your path toward homeownership and financial wealth without having a penny.

Your goal should always be realistic, tangible, and measurable. Set goals you know you can achieve. Have specific starting, middle, and ending points. Make sure you reward yourself incrementally throughout the process to keep yourself motivated and positive.

The perfect credit score is 850. With all of the credit reports I've looked at and the millions of dollars of loans that I have closed, I have never seen a perfect credit score. However, I've seen plenty of scores in the 600s, 700s, and 800s at all different financial levels. Take the time to set your individual BHAG. What is it that you want your credit report to say about you?

It's the American dream, God's vision, and your vision to be prosperous and in good standing. I call that *your credit destiny*. Your destination should be a place of comfort, security, and abundance. By taking the initial positive steps you are on your way to fulfilling your credit destiny. It's not always going to be an easy road. It's going to require discipline. It's going to require dedication. It's going to take some sacrifice, but at the end of the road, you'll have amazing rewards. You'll have confidence to know that what you want is at your fingertips and you will never have to worry again.

What do you want your credit destiny to be? What do you want to be able to do, have or achieve once you're in a strong financial position?

NOTES:

Chapter 2:

When You Know Better You Do Better

Before I share with you my experience and knowledge on how to set forth your credit and financial path, I feel it's important to share with you my background. I will share my successes and failures without bragging or shame. My life has been what it's been. Hopefully, you can take something from my experiences to improve an aspect of your financial future.

I grew up in a typical middle-class family in Schenectady, New York about 10 miles from the state capitol. Both of my parents were teachers and dabbled in small businesses from time to time with middling success and the occasional failure. One thing that was a constant throughout my childhood was that my parents were always homeowners. Until my young adulthood, I never knew what it was like to be a renter. I was always conditioned to own a house and followed that path as a young adult. My sister and I had a good childhood. We would take summer vacations to visit relatives or visit cities we hadn't been to before. We always had two or three cars—never luxury cars, but never jalopies, and we were never disillusioned that we were rich. We didn't live like *Good Times*, but we weren't living like *The Jeffersons* either.

Although we never discussed finances in the household, in doing research for this book, I found out that credit became a growing issue for my parents in the 1980s.

As my parents dabbled in side businesses and with the

rising costs of living, they began to rely more and more upon the use of credit cards. Things were a little different back then. Credit cards weren't so readily available but when used incorrectly were equally as dangerous. In 1985 we took a family summer vacation to Los Angeles, CA that was financed almost exclusively on credit cards. My father recently told me that for our 2 week trip it took almost 5 years for the cards to be completely paid off.

While my parents never had 'bad credit', the crunch of escalating bills did have some effect on their lifestyle as my sister and I started college a few years later and the eventual retirement of my father from the education system. It's not unique for families to get over their heads in revolving debt, but when discussed as a family financial issue, it can be a learning experience for future generations.

Credit reluctance was always instilled by my father, but it was without context. He never told us the good and the bad about credit. He just always said "Don't do it." The total extent of our credit education and discussions for my sister and I as young adults were "Don't mess with credit." However, as you will learn, having no credit is actually worse than having poor credit.

After graduating from high school, I went away to college, prepared to tackle the world and all it had to throw at me — and then I fell right into the trap. In the fall of 1988, I strolled into the student union at Winston-Salem State University and saw the tables for Visa, MasterCard, and Sears. Ignoring my father's advice, I went over to the tables and filled out the credit card applications. Within 30 days I had three credit cards in my mailbox for $500, $500 and $1000. Why would these companies give a college student with no credit history and no discernable income these credit cards?

This is the biggest mistake that young adults make every single year. Today, many credit card applications are in the orientation packages college students receive on day one or even in the pre-orientation packages sent to the home before school starts! Under-informed college students see the opportunity for fast, free money without realizing the repercussions they will feel for years to come.

Being the (somewhat) good son, I told my Dad that I had gotten a few credit cards but that I would be smart with them. He was annoyed, but he said, "Only use those for emergencies." I managed my spending ok for awhile—and then I splurged. I was working at a sporting goods store and we got our new shipment of warm-up suits and tennis rackets. So, I bought a new warm-up and of course I had to buy a matching pair of sneakers— I was looking good. I even bought a tennis racket. Here's the funny thing—I don't even play tennis! Of course I eventually maxed out my cards and my minimum monthly payments jumped from $18 to $72. Since I was a young college student with limited income and limited assets, that became a significant financial setback. And as you know, when it rains, it pours. My trusty car became less trustworthy. The repairs caused me to max out the Sears card. As my school work increased, my hours available to work decreased. Does any of this sound familiar?

My sister and I were in college at the same time, so with two children in college, I wasn't about to ask my parents for money to pay for my mistakes. It says in the Bible, 'Pride cometh before the fall.' That was the beginning of my first credit downfall.

Late payments became numerous, the phone calls were too much to take and the late fees compounded the problem. I had amassed a large amount of credit debt. As the years progressed I was able to chip away at the debt. It took me 5 years to pay those cards off, but not before my Visa and MasterCard were canceled. One of my favorite co-workers used to constantly joke with me that she saw the rise and fall of my credit.

I graduated from college in the summer of 1992, with poor credit and a poorer understanding of how it worked.. From my brief experience, my opinion about credit was if I don't use it, it can't hurt me. I didn't realize how wrong that was until a few years later when I decided to buy a car without any established credit, what I had from college was bad. While I was able to eventually secure financing, it was at a higher much rate and as well as a higher payment than it would have been had I understood that I should have been re-establishing and maintaining good credit.

A few years later, since I didn't have any credit card debt and my car payment was my only monthly obligation, I decided it was time to purchase a home. You'll see in Chapter 8 how you can benefit from my ignorance in waiting so long to purchase a home. I attended a First Time Homebuyers Seminar and was amazed at just how EASY it was going to be to purchase a home even without perfect credit. I fell into some common misconceptions about buying my first home.

- I thought I needed 20% down payment-WRONG.
- I thought I needed to have had perfect credit-

WRONG.

- I thought I couldn't afford a mortgage payment-WRONG.

I was able to own **_MY OWN HOME_** for what my rent was costing me. However easy it was, I still had to account for my previous credit mistakes. I ended up getting an FHA loan, which at the time had higher rates than conventional financing, and had to write a letter of explanation for my prior missteps.

The proudest moment of my life to that point was closing on that home. I had accomplished the American Dream, something I had always known as a child but was now experiencing as an adult. That proud moment really hit home later that afternoon when after showing my parents the house that I bought, my Mom cried as we were going to Wal-Mart to buy items for the home. To this day I don't know if those were tears of pride, or if she was just so happy I was taking her to her favorite place to shop, but I like to think they were for me.

I made sure I always made my mortgage payments on time but I still didn't understand credit completely and how to leverage the home as part of my overall financial goal setting and strategy. I still have great memories of that house. It was my biggest purchase to date, an accomplishment of a goal and should have been the first step towards building my individual wealth.

In the winter of 2001, my wife and I decided to purchase a newly constructed home closer to our jobs. Unfortunately, this would turn out to be one of the worst decisions of my life as it began an avalanche of financial difficulties. I made four key mistakes during this time period that, hopefully, you can learn from.

Mistake #1—We established a maximum sales price and a monthly payment that we could comfortably fit into our budget, but we fell in love with the house and emotion overrode logic. We overspent by purchasing a house $25,000 over our budget and exceeded our target mortgage payment by more than $300 a month. Budgeting and planning are keys to financial success regardless of your goals. When making a major purchase such as a home, establishing and sticking to your budget is extremely important regardless of other factors you may encounter.

- LESSON-NEVER FALL IN LOVE WITH REAL ESTATE!!

Mistake #2—We went into the loan process with a preconceived notion in mind of a 95%, 30-year fixed mortgage being the only option. It was far too conservative for that time and we ended up paying more than was necessary. My neighbors, who were more financially savvy than I was at the time, were paying $800 a month while I was paying over $1800.

- LESSON-ALWAYS KNOW AND UNDERSTAND YOUR OPTIONS!!

Mistake #3—Much to my surprise, I had a 680 credit score when the loan was done. So armed with that knowledge, I went out and financed some new furniture, a new big-screen television, and other electronics. Of course, to do this I used store credit cards. I had rapidly opened new revolving accounts and utilized my full available credit line. No payments for 2 years-no problem, right? __*WRONG!*__ My score dropped 60 points in 30 days.

- LESSON-AVOID STORE AND FINANCE COMPANY CREDIT CARDS!!

Mistake #4—At the time that we were purchasing the house, we both went through job changes. We were both laid off from our jobs. I transitioned into a new career, while my wife moved into a different position with a new company. In changing jobs, having to finance two newer cars, and armed with a one-year severance package into a commission-only business was far more challenging than I had anticipated. *When making a large financial decision, always have adequate reserves and a financial plan to support whatever decision you're making.* Things were okay for a while, but being relatively new to the mortgage business, sales were up and down and being in a commission only position there are always bare months. At one period my payments starting getting behind—first on small credit cards, then the furniture, then cars, and eventually the mortgage. Once the mortgage got behind it was a constant game of catch-up. There were good months income-wise and that would get us back afloat, but it was very difficult to get ahead. At the lowest point, we were 60 days late on the mortgage, 30 days late on the cars, and 30 days late on the credit cards, which resulted in a 496 credit score. I couldn't finance a box of Girl Scout cookies!

- LESSON-HAVE ADEQUATE RESERVES IN CASE 'LIFE HAPPENS'!!

I felt hypocritical advising clients on how to purchase a home when my financial house was in shambles. I was giving credit education but couldn't follow my own advice. I had a boss at the time that would classify bad credit borrowers as having "loser credit". It was difficult to sit across the table and hear her say that about other people and realizing she could have been talking about me.

In 2004, I attended a credit seminar for work and that's when the light bulb finally came on. Now I knew the formula, I just had to implement it. From that day forward, my goal was to improve my credit rating and share with as many people as possible the information that I had learned. However, in order to be able to teach with integrity, I had to get my finances in order. The constant credit and financial yo-yo at home had its affect on our marriage and eventually, we divorced. The next year, we sold the house and paid off most of the outstanding bills, following some financial challenges resulting from the divorce, I relocated to Miami and started fresh.

I was fortunate to have a house that my Grandfather gave me and after paying off some bills, I was able to get my credit score to a point where I could do a cash-out refinance on a sub prime loan, which is a mortgage that lenders typically give to customers who have poor credit at a much higher interest rate, to pay off the remainder of my bills. The first thing I did was pay off the high-balance credit limit lines and my finance company loans. Then I paid off, but left open, my revolving accounts, my auto loan and some student loans.

The damage had been done, so it took time for my score to rebound. There is no magic bullet when your credit is in a state of disrepair. However, as a result of diligently paying my bills on a monthly basis, my credit score jumped 70 points in six months.

In 2006, my recovery was 90 % complete. I was able to refinance my grandfather's old house one more time onto a conventional mortgage, save some money each month, get a little cash out, and purchase a condo in Florida three miles from the beach. Finally I was in a great place and life is good.

The old cliché goes—knowledge is power. And as the title of this chapter suggests, when you know better, then you ought to do better. Take a look at the big picture and educate yourself on market conditions when making large financial decisions. If you're credit is less than perfect, don't let pride get in the way of progress. Don't be afraid to ask for help. Learn from my mistakes.

I am not a business school graduate with any fancy degrees or titles. I'm not a millionaire talking theories and concepts. I'm speaking from real-life experiences—life's ups and downs that have affected me personally.

As we proceed toward your credit destiny, think about the following.

- What are you financial footsteps?
- What lessons could you learn from childhood and your early adult life?
- If you didn't have financial discussions with your parents, find out now what things were like and why.
- What are the key mistakes that you are determined to avoid and what are your keys to success?

NOTES:

Chapter 3:

Cash is King, Credit is the Queen

As the chapter title suggests, in America cash is king and credit is the queen. If you weren't fortunate enough to have a trust fund, a rich uncle, or an uncanny ability to pick six magical numbers out of the air and win the lottery, you have to rely on credit throughout life to achieve your financial goals. That's why credit is like a queen—the better you understand her, the happier you both will be.

Understand your credit scores. There are three traditional credit reporting bureaus with their own unique scoring models. However, the basics are consistent throughout each bureau. By definition, the credit score indicates the likelihood of a borrower going 90 days late on a future loan.

Various factors determine a borrower's credit score. Each factor carries a certain weight of percentage on what determines a borrower's credit score. The credit score can be broken down into the following percentages:

35% of the score is based on the borrower's recent payment history. This history is broken into three components:

- Recency—the length of time that has lapsed since the delinquency. If an individual has a late payment on their credit report, initially that delinquency will have a very negative effect on their credit score. As the delinquency ages, it will have a lessening negative effect on the score. Use the three categories below to gauge how severe a recent late payment will affect the score.

- o 0-6—months a very negative effect on the individual's credit.
- o 7-23—months a moderate negative effect on the individual's credit.
- o 24+ months—that's when a delinquency drops out of having a negative effect.
- Frequency—the frequency of delinquent payments. How often a person was 30 / 60 / 90 / 120 days late
- Severity—how delinquent a person was: 30 / 60 / 90 / 120 days late.

The combination of these factors together will affect this portion of the credit score.

15% of the score is determined by the amount of credit history. The credit scoring bureaus are looking at much review for the length of time a person has had an account. If a person has four credit cards that have been open for two years each, the credit score formula sees this as having an eight year history. Some people would advise to close accounts in order to improve a credit score. **THIS IS INCORRECT.** Do not close out your old accounts. It will not enhance your scores. What it will do is negatively affect your credit history and the score drops.

Warning! Keep in mind that when new credit card accounts are opened they affect the history of other existing credit cards. For example, say you have one credit card that has been open with a six-year history, then open two more credit lines. Now the credit score module sees three cards as if they've been open for two years each. You've eliminated 3 years of your credit history that can save you money by you having a higher score which means more favorable rates and terms!!

30% of the credit score is based on the <u>debt balance</u> versus the <u>high credit limit</u> of each <u>revolving type of trade line</u>. There are two thresholds in this category that negatively affects a person's score.

- 50% of debt balance versus the high credit limit has a moderately negative affect to the score.
- 75% of the debt balance to the high credit limit has a stronger negative affect to the score.

Here's the key—debt balances kept at or below 33% of the high credit limit as reported to the credit bureaus will positively affect the credit score. Remember, this section is worth 30% of 850 possible points on a credit score.

Another interesting note in this category regarding home equity lines—there's a certain dollar amount when the credit score formula looks at a home equity line as a <u>revolving account</u> rather than an <u>installment loan</u>. While we don't exactly know what that number is, we understand that if someone takes out a credit line in the range of $0 - $20,000, there is a high chance that the formula will look at the home equity line as a revolving account. We also understand that somewhere in the neighborhood of greater than $25,000, the credit formula will look at an equity line as an installment loan. This is very important, because a revolving account with a debt balance above 50 or 75 % will be viewed negatively in a person's credit rating.

Recently, I was talking to someone who had a 698 credit score and went out and leased a luxury vehicle and took out what they *thought* was a $10,000 home equity loan. Thirty days later they were reviewing their credit and their credit score was a 602! They had lost 96 points in thirty days!! Why is that? The report showed two maxed out revolving accounts — $10,000 on the credit line was reported as revolving rather than installment and even though they had taken the loan as an equity line of credit, it appeared that it was not secured to the real estate because of the balance.

10% of your score is determined by the type of trade-lines that you have. The credit scoring formula likes to see a mix of type of trade lines a person has. However, *finance company credit cards (i.e. store credit cards to finance electronics, furniture, etc.) are not viewed favorably in the credit scoring model*. Statistics bear out that individuals with finance company credit cards have a higher likelihood of having delinquent payments. The same bears true for those who have personal unsecured loans with finance companies.

10% of your score is determined by inquiries. People can relax a little bit about getting their credit pulled. A total of 85 points can be earned or lost with inquiries. In addition, the credit score model is only looking for inquiries within the past twelve months, and it allows 7 to 10 inquiries for that twelve month period. When a score is hit for inquiries, it is hit 5 to 15 points each. However, the credit scoring models have been programmed to recognize mortgage and auto-loan related pulls, knowing that there could be several within a short period. The model has been altered to allow a thirty-day buffer for re-pulls of mortgage-related inquiries.

Everybody knows someone who has struggled during or after a divorce and whose score is suffering from bills that were supposed to be paid off by the spouse but were not. Unfortunately, there is nothing that can be done in that situation to immediately improve their score simply based on that fact. The individual can submit a 100-word explanation of the situation that will show up on their credit report; however, this will not affect the score up or down.

A note on credit counseling services—in the past, credit scoring bureaus frowned upon consumer credit counseling (CCCS) more and treated it as if it were a bankruptcy. Now these regulations have loosened up a bit. Believe it or not, it can sometimes *worsen* an individual's score when they pay off old collections. Paying an older collection can actually lower the score by refreshing the recency of a collection. If it were to be left unpaid it would continue to get older and older and thus lessening the negative recency effect.

If you are in a situation where a collection needs to be paid off before a lender will work with a loan, ***make sure that you have the collection paid at the closing***. That way, any re-pulled credit reports before the loan closing will not have a negative impact by refreshing an older collection. Do not, however, ignore paying your collections for the long term effect it may have on your score. Unless you are in a situation where you need to close out a loan and you need your score to be a certain number, go ahead and get those collections paid and out of the way.

To sum it up, what do you want to do to help your

score?

- Keep your balances at or below 33% when they're reported to the credit bureaus.
- You can increase your revolving credit limit without having your credit score re-pulled by the creditor.
- Take a look at what stage a recent delinquency is in and when it may move to a lesser category.
- Protect yourself in advance from damaged credit resulting from a divorce.
- Most importantly, pay your bills on time.

Things to avoid that will hurt your score:
- Do not open finance company credit cards ever.
- Do not open new credit before a new loan.
- Do not pay off old collections right before re-pulling credit.
- Do not open small home equity lines.
- Do not close old credit accounts.

While complex and confusing, the credit score models are set up in such a way that by making timely payments and paying off debts, you are never more than two years away from a decent credit score. Bad things happen to good people all the time. Contrary to popular belief your credit score is not a reflection of who you are—it is a reflection of who you were. *You can change that and start fulfilling your credit destiny one day and one bill at a time.*

At my seminars I always do the following exercise. I ask the audience to close their eyes and envision their credit destiny. What do you want your credit report to say about you? When you've achieved that ultimate goal, what does that look like? The visual image I talk about is the dream sequence at the end of *Titanic* when Jack and Rose walk into the Grand Ballroom and everyone is there to welcome them into a world of luxury. That is how you're treated when you ultimately fulfill your credit destiny.

- What have you learned about credit scoring and formulas that you can put into practice in your life immediately?
- What 5 action steps can you take in the next 60 days to rapidly improve your score?

NOTES:

_____

_____

_____

_____

_____

_____

_____

_____

_____

_____

_____

_____

_____

_____

_____

_____

_____

_____

Chapter 4:

Get Your Ka-Ching Before Your Bling-Bling

The fundamentals of practical, disciplined, and effective financial planning are based in assessing your basic wants versus needs. Wealth-building principals are all built on short-term sacrifice for long-term gain. Credit and home ownership are the cornerstones of long-term financial stability.

The first thing you want to do is outline your fixed costs—housing, utilities, communication, food, and transportation. Transportation is always a funny thing. A lot of times people just need to get from point A to point B, but choose the most luxurious way to get there.

While out recently, my date began to talk about what she had done and who she knew, what she had, her LUXURY APARTMENT she was _renting_ and we started talking about cars. She very proudly told me that she was the owner of a brand new BMW-3 Series. With equal parts pride and probably indignation, I told her I was the proud owner of a 1997 paid for 1-Series. It's just my opinion, but to me there is nothing more depressing than to see an expensive car in an apartment complex. It's foolish to buy depreciating assets, expensive clothes, cars, or furniture before appreciating assets—a home, an IRA, or other investments. Don't own a Land Rover and no land!!

Outline your variable costs. Look at your entertainment,

your shopping, your travel, etc. Take a hard, critical look at what are your core and emotional needs. Once you determine your core needs and maybe one or two emotional needs as well, you need to take time to set up your financial priorities.

One of the biggest obstacles when assessing your wants versus your needs is the classic emotional need. An emotional need is when you see something you really want and you classify it as a need. "I need that Fendi bag." "I need that BMW." "I need that shopping weekend." I developed a concept that still had that emotional feeling of satisfaction while still maintaining your budget and your discipline on your long-term goals.

It's called *"Buy it in your mind."* Imagine how much more satisfying your new purse will look on the counter in the kitchen of your new home. Imagine how nice your car will look in your driveway, instead of an apartment parking lot. Imagine how satisfying it will be to come home from shopping and put your clothes away in the closet of your new house. Buy it in your mind, claim it, and make the decision that it will be yours—but only in its due time.

I recently had a conversation with a minister about some of the financial challenges in his congregation. He told me he started his Christian financial counseling sessions the same way every time. He said financial issues are always founded on one of two principals. Either you have an **earning problem** or a **spending problem**. That was so simple that it was profound to me. Either you don't make enough money, or you spend too much of what you don't have! *Most of the time it seems like the former, but in fact it's the latter.* Track your spending for a week, month or 3 months and see where your hard earned money goes. I guarantee you'll be surprised.

Whether it's a budget, a diet, an exercise regimen, or whatever it is that you do that forces some level of sacrifice, it is human nature to fight it at some point. You have to reward yourself incrementally to keep yourself motivated. Your rewards should be tangible, but reasonable. Always budget for your reward and your reward should be a celebration of your accomplishment and motivation to keep moving forward.

- What are your spending patterns?
- Can you identify your wants, your core needs and your emotional needs?
- What 3 things have you identified about your spending that you can change in the next 30 days?

NOTES:

Chapter 5:

Building Blocks of Finance

Hopefully by now you have determined that you are committed to having an ideal credit score and are planning for a wealthy and prosperous life. One of the fundamentals of savings is the principal of compounding interest.

For example, $50 a month invested in a savings account at 3%, which by the way is a very low percentage by today's standard, compounding annually after 15 years, that account will be worth over $11,000. $150 a month at the same rate over the same period would equate to more than $34,000. $500 a month would net you a whopping *$114,000*.

Even starting relatively small, a committed savings plan can increase your financial standing and net worth before you realize it. Most financial planners and advisors would tell you, ideally, you should save a minimum of 10% of your income on a weekly, monthly, and annual basis.

As you saw in a previous chapter, 80% of your credit score is determined in some way by your usage of credit. It's necessary that you use credit and utilize it in a smart way. Having no credit is WORSE than having bad credit.

Have a monthly credit card expense—whether it's groceries, dinner, paying a bill—you have to use your credit. Keep it manageable and something you can pay every month. Make sure you always keep it to less than 33% of the high credit limit. Leaving a card unused has the same affect on your credit score as not having it.

Do not **ever, ever, ever** apply for a store credit card to qualify for a giveaway. These are huge credit traps. *Store credit cards = finance companies and finance company cards = lower credit scores.*

When you move, always double check with your service providers for the final bill, and request a paid-in-full letter clearing your account of any outstanding balances. This is one of the most common sources of unknown collections. Of course, pay your bills on time, but if you are having problems, then be proactive and get in front of it. Often, if arranged before hand, credit card companies may take a lesser payment and not report you late on your credit report, as long as you make good on the next billing period.

The formula of a near-perfect credit score all the time is as simple as 3 – 2 – 1. By maintaining a ratio of three installment accounts—for example, an auto loan, student loan, personal loan from a banking institution but not a finance company— two revolving accounts—a credit card or home equity line of credit of less than $25,000—and one mortgage all paid on time with the proper balance to credit limit ratio will give you a near-perfect credit score almost every time. An abundance of one over the other will result in the scoring models reading your credit as out of balance and can lower your score. Start early with 3 – 2 – 1 in mind and maintain that ratio throughout your financial lifetime.

Here are several debt reducing strategies to follow:

- A tried and true formula for paying down debt is paying small to big. This is a good way to eliminate debts if you're not saddled with excessively high interest rates. The basic concept is focusing your extra money to pay off your smallest bills first, and once that is paid, roll that money into the next highest, and so forth, until you pay them all off. This is a great way to go if you aren't already upside down in debt or if you have a while to clear up the debt that you've accumulated.

- Another plan is the ten dollar a day plan. Set aside $10.00 a day, either by reducing your spending or incurred savings, to apply toward your debt. By doing this $10.00 a day, you will save $300 a month. Over the span of a year, you will save over $3600!

- For those of you who are extra ambitious, live 30% below your means for twelve to 24 months. By allocating all that extra money towards paying off your debt, you will be amazed at how quickly you can reduce your debt and improve your credit score.

- Always pay additional towards principal whenever possible. Bi-weekly payments versus monthly payments will pay things down much quicker. Everyone's situation is unique. Take the time to examine your finances and determine what plan works for you.

No matter how you choose to establish your credit and budgeting plan, starting doing it today. Go to www.annualcreditreport.com and get your free copies of your credit report from each bureau.

- Now that you know the formulas what action steps can you take to improve your score 40 points in the next 60 days?
- What are 3 areas that you can make changes in your spending or savings habits in the next 30 days ?

NOTES:

Chapter 6:

Protecting Your Credit

Imagine this—you are sitting across the desk from your mortgage loan officer, you just filled out the loan application with confidence because you know you paid all your bills on time. You saved money to pay for your closing costs. You have even seen the house of your dreams and it is in your price range. The American Dream is at your fingertips. Your heart sinks in your chest when the smile disappears from the lender's face as he reveals your credit report shows numerous open accounts that have not been paid and you are not eligible for a loan.

As you review your credit report, you are flabbergasted at what you see. Delinquencies from stores you've never been to. Cell phone collections from companies you have never used. And you do not even know what you could think to buy for $900 at Victoria's Secret. You have just become a statistic.

In recent years, identity theft reports have increased dramatically. In fact, it is the fastest growing crime in the U. S. today. In 2006, 8.9 million adults were victims of identity fraud or theft. The average amount per victim is over $6,000. When the individual takes the time to resolve their own identity theft issues, an estimated $13,500 is incurred, including an average of 40 work hours to rectify that situation.

While the loss or theft of wallets, purses, checkbooks, or credit cards are a factor, almost half of identity fraud and theft victims know their perpetrators—friends, neighbors, in-home employees, and family members are most of the identity thieves in America. 47% of victims can identity the source of the compromised information, and 36% can identify the person who committed the fraud.

Only 30% of identity fraud cases were Internet related. Be smart about usage of credit cards online. Look for the "lock" symbol in the lower right-hand corner, which reflects encrypted websites that can be trusted. The old saying is "an ounce of prevention is worth a pound of cure" applies to your finances and credit management is no exception.

AnnualCreditReport.com is a vital tool to your credit management. By reviewing your credit report on an annual basis, you can see the activity, your credit score, your payment history, and any items that appear to be there that should not. Act on those items immediately.

Make a small investment in a safe to keep your most valuable items—passport, social security card and so forth— out of the hands of thieves. The security of that safe is worth priceless peace of mind.

Record your account numbers and passwords in a safe place, and do as many paperless transactions as possible to avoid the possibility of your personal information being compromised.

Protecting yourself from identity thieves is paramount to achieving your financial goals. I firmly believe that you should protect your credit more than cash. You can always make more money but recovering and correcting your credit can be a long and tenuous process.

Here is some guidance on prevention and what you

should do if you suspect you've been victimized.

Be smart and don't leave printed personal and/or financial information lying around the home. Seems like common sense, doesn't it? You'd be surprised. More often than not, identity thieves are friends and relatives of the victim who get their personal information off-line.

Shred bank, credit statements, and credit card offers before throwing them away. Shredders are very affordable today and can be purchased for less than $50.

Don't mail checks from your home mailbox. Instead, drop them off at a U. S. mailbox or at the Post Office.

Take advantage of online banking and check your balance frequently. Reviewing your personal financial statements at least once a week, you will be able to spot fraud sooner if it happens. Catching a fraud early on minimizes the damage thieves can do and usually results in less time and money spent resolving problems.

Be tech-savvy and cover your tracks. When trying to avoid potential identity theft, think like a crook and close off any potential gaps. Install a firewall and buy virus-protection software. If you dispose of a personal computer, remove your data from the hard drive with a wipe utility program.

Be smart about choosing your passwords. When choosing your passwords, don't use the same password for all of your accounts. Avoid using your Social Security number or any parts of it, your name, your mom's name, maiden name, birth date, middle name, pet's name, or consecutive guessable numbers for passwords.

What to you do if identity theft strikes? Call the credit bureaus immediately and get their help.

- <u>Equifax</u> 1-800-685-1111
- <u>Experian</u> 1-888-397-3742
- <u>Trans Union</u> 1-800-888-4213

Lock thieves out of your accounts by changing all of your passwords and account access information. Establish new PIN numbers for your ATM and debit cards. Report the crimes to all relevant authorities. Call the local Police Department and file a police report noting all of the accounts and amounts that have been compromised. Report all your fraudulent transactions to creditors. Contact them for any accounts that have been tampered with or opened without your knowledge. Be sure to put your complaints in writing. Ask each creditor to provide you and your local Police Department with copies of the documents showing fraudulent transactions. Keep a log of everything you do to resolve problems. Write down each person's name, title, and phone number in case you need to follow-up or refer to them in later correspondence.

It's not the easiest thing to deny when you're faced with a friend or relative who is in a financial bind and they ask you to help them out and co-sign for them or if they can put a bill in your name—just say no. Never, ever co-sign. Remember, credit is the one thing that it's okay to be selfish with. Don't let someone else's financial issues derail your short and long-term goals. If they weren't responsible when it was their credit on the line, why would it be any better with yours? If the bills don't get paid, it's your credit that gets ruined. When you sign, you become just as responsible. Co-signed accounts are scored the same as individually opened accounts.

Maintaining a good credit history requires hard work, dedication and discipline. Don't let the criminal or foolish actions of others deter you from your destiny.

- What 3 steps can you take to better protect your identity?
- Where are gaps in your data security that an identity thief can exploit if you don't correct it immediately?

NOTES:

Chapter 7:

The ABC's of Credit Repair

The realities of life are that sometimes bad credit happens to good people. You get sick, laid off, divorced, there's a family illness, or you just fall on hard financial times. There are circumstances beyond your control every day that can cause you to get off the path. Here's the good news, though—you are not alone.

In the 1980s, my favorite football team, the Washington Redskins, was a dynasty—appearing in three Super Bowls, winning two before adding another championship in 1993. Head Coach Joe Gibbs was well known as a strong Christian man and well respected for his integrity and leadership skills. He became a Hall of Fame Coach by leading these teams to championships. But during the peak of his professional career, his financial house was in ruins. He had gotten into a bad real estate investment deal and when the housing market in Oklahoma went south, he ended up in a tremendous amount of debt, losing $30,000 a month. He didn't file bankruptcy as his partners had. He leaned on his faith and the good fortunes of others and after four and a half years, he had finally paid back all the debt.

The moral of the story is even when the situation looks bleak or impossible, there is always a way back.

I've said for many years the two things you have ultimate control over are your weight and your credit. If you have an extra chin or a 498 credit score, it didn't happen over night, so the first step is realizing there are no quick fixes. I'm not going to sugar coat it. Recovering from a bad credit score can be a long, difficult — and depending on the level of trouble you've had — an expensive experience. But the light at the end of the tunnel is no longer a train.

As with anything positive you set out to do in life, there are always pitfalls and traps you have to overcome. Creating your credit destiny is no different. Here are some of the common traps and how to avoid them.

The Quick Fix

Building or rebuilding credit takes time. There are all sorts of companies that will offer to fix your credit in 30 days or remove all bad information from your credit, or even give you a new identity and a fresh credit start. Many of these companies are either scams or promoting illegal activity. Even the legitimate ones are expensive--$800 or more and can take years for them to clear things up. Most legitimate credit repair services charge you a premium for doing what you can do for yourself. What costs more — $800 to a third party, or paper, envelopes, and stamps? For $800 you can buy a computer and printer and write your own letters! There are many non-profit agencies and consumer credit counseling services that will help you clean up your credit for little or no cost.

The Short Cut

Co-signing on other's existing accounts may seem like a good way to build a quick credit history, but banks and lenders see through this transparent attempt to show more of a credit history than you actually have. In September 2007, the credit scoring models will be modified to exclude authorized user accounts from counting towards your credit score. By starting the right way early on, you will be able to set your credit destiny in motion.

Quickie Credit Cards

There are secured credit cards that can help build your credit rating if used properly, but again there are plenty of predators out there waiting to take advantage of you with higher rates and outlandish fees. Go to www.cardwatch.com or www.Bankrate.com for cards with favorable rates and manageable fees.

Here's the good news, there is no more satisfying feeling than to pay that last bill off or knowing a collection that has been hanging over your head for years is never going to be a worry for you again. The emotional freedom of either being debt-free or on a solid path to a great credit score is a euphoric feeling beyond words.

The first step in credit repair is to acknowledge your situation, commit to resolving your outstanding debts and make that your most important goal. Resolve to make it a part of your lifestyle to never have bad credit again. Stay diligent and make sacrifices for the long-term benefit. Monitor your progress, occasionally pull your credit from AnnualCreditReport.com, or utilize MyFico.com. Start slowly and have a plan of attack.

First, dispute all the negative items on your credit report. Use the Fair Credit Reporting Act to your benefit. Once you dispute an item, the credit bureaus have a 30-day time period that they have to respond to you or delete that item from your credit report. Know who and what you have to pay. Key mistakes are often made by ignoring or giving up on a company when you can't reach someone. Over 90% of credit reports contain outdated or erroneous information. One of the biggest myths and misconceptions that people have about credit is that after seven years all bad credit goes away. The truth of the matter is seven years from the last date it was reported is when it drops off your credit report. But if you have a debt that is six years and eleven months old, if it gets reported, buckle up and get comfortable, you have another seven long years to wait.

As discussed in a previous chapter, pay off the smaller bills you have the money for first. Use a graduated scale, paying off the lowest balance to the highest balance to pay off all your bills. Be proactive and call and/or write every creditor and ask for the current pay-off amount and possibly even a payment plan. Ask about a negotiated settlement and document every conversation. Make sure you emphasize that you want to pay the outstanding debt as soon as possible and are open to ways to do that. Do as much via email and fax as possible.

Part of your recovery is re-establishing your credit while repairing it. While data remains on your credit report for seven years from the last reported date—ten years for bankruptcies and public records—remember, you are never more than two years away from a great credit score.

Recovery can be summed up in three simple steps: **say,** **pay,** and **stay.**

Say out loud to yourself that you are going to commit to

getting your credit on track. Repeat this affirmation daily to give yourself power and pride in reaching your goal.

__Pay__ your past debtors and your current bills in a timely manner. Training yourself with this new pattern will make it impossible to go against this nature in the future and ensure your positive credit destiny.

__Stay__ diligent in your quest for good credit. Don't let obstacles—and there will be obstacles—stand in your way. Anything worth having requires hard work, so be undeterred by anything that keeps you from your goal. Repeat this mantra to yourself weekly, daily, or as a motivation before each call to a creditor.

Dealing with collection agencies is a part of repairing and re-establishing credit that can be considered a necessary evil. Collectors have the well-earned reputation of being bullies, rude, threatening, irrational, and just down-right mean. Fortunately, the Fair Debt Collection Practices Act gives you governmental protection against some of the illegal tactics used by collectors in trying to settle a debt.

Here are some collection tactics they can and cannot implement:

- A collector may contact you in person, by mail, telephone, or fax. However, a debt collector may not contact you at an inconvenient time or place, such as before 8 a.m. or after 9 p.m. unless you agree.
- Debt collectors may not contact you at work if the collector knows your employer disapproves of such contact.

- You can stop a debt collector from contacting you by writing a letter to the collection agency telling them to stop. Once they receive the letter, they may not contact you again except to say that there will be no further contact or to notify you that the debt collector intends to take some specific action. However, even though you send this letter, you still owe that debt and should pay it in order to secure your financial destiny.

- A debt collector can not contact any body else unless you designate an attorney for them to contact. Collectors are prohibited from contacting these third parties more than once. In most cases, the collector may not tell anyone other than you and your attorney that you owe money.

- Within five days after you are first contacted the collector must send you a written notice telling you the amount of money that you owe, the name of the creditor to whom you owe the money, and what action to take if you do not believe you owe the money.

- A collection agency may not contact you if within 30 days after you receive that written notice you send the collection agency a letter stating that you do not owe the money. However, they can continue to report that on your credit report until the account has been settled or the dispute has been resolved.

- Debt collectors are prohibited from harassing, pressing, abusing you or any third parties that they contact. For example, debt collectors may not use threats of violence or harm, threaten to publish a list of consumers who refuse to pay their debts, except to a credit bureau, use obscene or profane language or repeatedly call to annoy you.

- Debt collectors can not falsely imply that they are attorneys or government representatives. They can not falsely imply that you've committed a crime or falsely represent that they operate or work for a credit bureau.

- Debt collectors can not misrepresent or inflate the amount of your debt or indicate that papers sent to you are legal forms when they are not. They can not indicate that papers are *not* legal forms when they are.

- Debt collectors can not tell you that you'll be arrested if you do not pay your debts. They may not give false credit information about you to anyone, including a credit bureau. They also may not send you anything that looks like an official document from a court or government agency when it's not, or use a false name.

If you have a problem with a collection agency and you feel they have violated your rights or any of the laws, report the problem to your State's Attorney General Office and to the Federal Trade Commission. Many states have their own debt collection laws and your Attorney General's Office can help you determine your rights.

As part of my Controlling Your Credit Destiny Credit Repair Kit, I have prepared some templates of letters that you can use to send to the collection agencies, credit bureaus, and other creditors in an effort to clear up your credit report. These letters have been used numerous times and are just as effective as the letters that credit repair companies charge you $500, $600, or $700 to produce.

BANKRUPTCY

If your situation is dire and you're in a hole that you cannot realistically work your way out of, there is always the option of filing bankruptcy. Bankruptcy should always be looked at as a last resort—not a bail out. Know the ramifications on your possibility to get a future mortgage, car loan, personal loan, insurance, or even a job. Bankruptcy filing hit an all-time high in 2005, as it was misused and abused as debt relief for poor decisions that people made.

There are two kinds of personal bankruptcy. Chapter 7 Bankruptcy represents a "fresh start." This can be filed every six years. However, delinquent child support, taxes, spousal support, or student loans cannot be included. It allows for all other debts to be completely forgiven. The downside is that it is looked upon more harshly by banks and lending institutions. Property can be reclaimed based on value and the time of filing from the purchase. Consult with a bankruptcy attorney for specific details.

The other option is a Chapter 13 Bankruptcy. This is looked upon as a "make good" or debt re-organization bankruptcy. It buys time from creditors as they cannot pursue you as long as you maintain the payment schedule predetermined by the courts. Qualifications are a source of income and an ability to pay debts in the next 60 months. Most times you can keep your property in a Chapter 13. Chapter 13 can halt foreclosure and repossession. You can actually purchase a house while in a Chapter 13 bankruptcy. It has to be an FHA loan and you need bank and trustee approval to pursue financing. It's more credit-friendly long term since you will have a court-monitored repayment plan in place you must commit to and stick to that plan.

There are two outcomes from a Chapter 13 Bankruptcy. It can be discharged or dismissed. A discharged bankruptcy means that you abided by the court's instructions, made your payments on time, and have reached the end of your bankruptcy proceedings. A dismissed Chapter 13 bankruptcy means that you did not fulfill your obligations to the courts and the court no longer recognizes your bankruptcy as valid. Banks and lending institutions look far more favorably upon a *discharged* bankruptcy than a *dismissed* bankruptcy.

When you file bankruptcy, it is not the end of the world. One of the first loans I ever did when I got in the mortgage business was from a gentleman who had filed bankruptcy one year before. His credit score was a 601. He was recently out of a bad divorce, had filed Chapter 13, and had a little bit of re-established credit. He had a good job, making middle-class income. I was able to get him approved for a loan, but he got a higher rate on his mortgage than a conventional mortgage. However, a year later I refinanced him and his credit score was in the 660s. Two years later I did a loan for him and his new wife and his credit score had gone up to a 710. Recently, I refinanced that loan for them so they could take some cash out and his credit score was in the 750s. In just a short period of time, by making smart credit decisions, keeping his balances low and by paying his bills in a timely manner, he went from filing bankruptcy to having a credit score in the mid 700s in only a few years.

Regardless of the path you choose to follow—either a payment plan, bankruptcy, paying a credit repair service or consumer credit counseling—make sure you educate yourself on the positives and negatives of each option and how it works for your unique situation. Don't let anyone tell you what's best for you. That is a very personal decision and it only directly affects you. Whatever you choose, act decisively with conviction, stay the course, and follow-up until you've got everything on track and you've secured your credit destiny.

- What's your plan? Outline how you will repair your credit and commit to it.
- Remember SAY, PAY, STAY and make it as much a part of your daily routine as brushing your teeth.
- What are your goals for credit repair in the next 3-6 months?

NOTES:

Chapter 8:

Homeownership Done Right

Homeownership—the American Dream. Simply put, home ownership is a key component in building wealth. All of which you have read to this point about the importance of credit, and how having a positive credit report can have a significant impact on your financial life comes to a zenith right here.

By starting homeownership at an early stage in your financial life, you have laid down the most important fundamental footstep towards building wealth.

The first thing I teach in my home ownership seminars is to develop amnesia. Forget everything you've ever heard about someone else's experience in buying a home. Each situation is unique, there is no such thing as one size fits all in purchasing a home. Based on my years of experience and millions of dollars in funded loans, I will dispel some myths and provide some insider insights on how to have all the power in speaking with your lender.

Down payment requirements are a thing of the past. Current wages versus the cost of living and inflation do not support saving 5%, 10%, or 20% for a down payment at a very early stage in life. Thankfully, that is no longer a requirement to achieve the American Dream. All major mortgage lenders have 100% financing programs for first time home buyers.

Fannie Mae and Freddie Mac, the agencies that buy most conventional mortgages, both have 100% options. For example, Fannie Mae has a program called "My Community." It is a 100% financing mortgage, meaning no money is required to be put down from the borrower. You can do a 30-year or a 40-year term and you can have reduced private mortgage insurance, which is required on all loans higher than 80% loan to value. Until 2007, PMI was looked upon as a negative but legislation was recently passed that makes it tax deductible for individuals earning less than $100,000 per year.

Another option is FHA, which has a 97% financing program with a 100% financing program pending. Down payment assistance programs are available to pay for the down payment or closing costs. In addition, you can get a gift from a friend, relative or qualified non-profit organization. Also, FHA has a program commonly called the 'kiddie condo' program. As a college student (whether you have income or not!) a parent or guardian can be a co-borrower for you on a purchase as a non-occupant and you can begin homeownership and generate rental revenue from your roommates as they help you build your financial foundation. This is a PHENOMENAL program, consult a mortgage professional for more details.

My vision for you or your child is to have your college diploma in one hand, a job offer letter in your other hand, and you closing on a home within 30 days. Loan programs are set up for that exact scenario to happen with no money down from the borrower. Today, more so than ever, lending guidelines are very favorable for young homeowners. For example, did you know that lenders consider education as employment? Let's say you graduate with a teaching degree and are offered a job by the local department of education.

Before you even START YOUR JOB, your diploma plus your offer letter is enough to get you approved for a mortgage to purchase a house with NO MONEY DOWN!

It is just this simple, the sooner you buy, the better off you are long-term. There is no other way to put this—paying rent is simply wasting money.

When you have had prior credit issues it will not prevent you from buying a house. With 6 to 12 months of a strong payment history and all delinquent accounts paid off, you should be in the position to get a conventional (Fannie Mae/ Freddie Mac) or FHA mortgage at market rates.

One thing you will have to do, however, is prepare a credit explanation letter to explain what happened and what you will do to prevent it from happening again. It needn't be much more than one or two paragraphs, but it's always good to end with: "I realize the importance of establishing and maintaining a positive credit history, and understand meeting my monthly mortgage obligation is necessary to maintain a positive rating." Underwriters love that line.

If you're like most people you are not going to be able to afford your dream home right out of the gate. The Late R&B singer Luther Vandross had a famous song *A House is Not a Home*. He's singing about coming home to a house filled with love and loved ones creating a sense of home. Well, in homeownership the same concept applies. A house is just sticks and bricks—a home is what you make it. While your first home may not have you living in the lap of luxury, you have taken an important step in securing your long-term financial future.

What to look for: For your first home, look for a house in an emerging neighborhood. This is a great way to build equity. Go to your local Chamber of Commerce and find out what areas are in revitalization zones. Another great place to build equity quickly is to buy a house that is <u>new construction</u> it in an early phase. Getting in on the ground level almost guarantees appreciation of your assets. Builders typically increase sales prices 5 to 10% per phase.

There are still some opportunities for foreclosure buy-outs or foreclosure sales. It is a very tough market to crack, but you will find the occasional deal. Educate yourself before going down this road so that way you don't end up buying somebody else's mess.

What to avoid: New construction builder close-outs. The builder will throw a bunch of perks your way such as paid <u>closing costs</u>, new furniture, gift cards to Home Depot but realize, your purchase price is already at the top of the market for your development and there is not much room for quick appreciation. Unless you are exceptionally handy or have money for constant repairs and upgrades, avoid fixer-uppers. They can get very expensive very quickly. Try to avoid lease-to-own, unless your credit dictates this, don't enter into this type of deal. You'll always end up spending more money. And I can't stress this enough—never get emotionally attached. Don't fall in love from the curb. It will cost you more money.

Homeownership is not an emotional decision—it's a financial decision and needs to be looked at from a logical and budgetary stand-point. Once you are in the house then you can make it your home.

There are two payment options when you get a

mortgage—fixed rate or adjustable.

Fixed rate loans are stable, secure and you know what your rate and payment are going to be for the next 15, 20, 30, or 40 years. A 30-year, fixed-rate mortgage is the Coca Cola or the General Motors of mortgages. It's solid, it's reliable, you know what you're getting—no surprises. The downside is rates are often higher than on an adjustable-rate mortgage. You usually have to pay your taxes and your insurance as part of your monthly payment and often times you'll have private mortgage insurance since typically you are doing one loan vs. a piggyback loan to avoid PMI.

The adjustable-rate mortgage or ARM is a risk-reward loan. With and ARM your interest rate is fixed for a period of time but will adjust monthly, semi-annually or annually for the term of the loan afterward. An ARM could be Microsoft or it could be Enron. Consumers have to educate themselves. Know what your short-term goals are. We'll talk exit strategies later, but always have one.

You hear a lot recently about interest-only loans. Are they good or are they bad? Well, that depends. The upside is your rate and payments are often lower so there are more ways to get to your desired outcome. There are usually more options and you can customize your loan to fit your scenario and build equity faster than a fixed rate.

Potential downsides include you can get caught in a down cycle and rates could be higher when it's time to refinance. Interest-only can also hurt you in a depreciating market, which is uncommon. Be careful and know what you're signing before you sign your closing documents. The high numbers of foreclosures in 2007 were from under-informed adjustable rate mortgage customers.

A lot of sub prime customers, short term ARM customers and <u>Pay-Option ARM</u> customers saw their payments jump 20%-100% when their loans adjusted after the fixed rate period. They didn't have an exit strategy to fall back on when the market turned.

Another wonderful thing about homeownership is that the U. S. Government, at the federal, state, and local levels, are invested in your real estate success. There are numerous programs out there for each state and most city municipalities that offer large sums of money as grants, gifts, or loans. In addition, there are plenty of non-profit organizations with money they HAVE TO give away in order to keep their funding.

Start by contacting your state, city or county's housing or urban development office to see what programs they have for first-time homebuyers or by visiting <u>www.mortgagegrants.</u><u>com</u> for information on down payment assistance programs available nationwide. Not all of them have stringent income requirements—some allow up to 140% of the area median income. For example, in the State of Florida, Miami Dade County offers up to $80,000 and an additional $10,000 from the State of Florida, plus another 6% of the purchase price from a different county agency, all for down-payment or closing costs assistance. That is a ***<u>lot of money</u>*** that makes homeownership a reality where it may not have been otherwise possible.

Perhaps in no other industry does your credit score have a financial impact on you than in homeownership. There are really two categories of loans—prime or sub-prime. Credit score requirement differences can be as slight as 20 points, but financially, it can be light years. Your prime or conventional loans always have lower rates; you have more options; you have more power to determine your loan; and you have the ability to shop for the best product and rates.

Interest rates usually have a variance of ½% to 1% from lender to lender for the same exact loan. However you have more controls over fees that you are charged, no pre-payment penalties, and these loans are usually highly regulated.

Typically, to qualify for a "prime" loan you have to have a credit score of at least 620. If you are below 620, then you are probably looking at doing a sub-prime loan. Sub-prime loans have higher rates, which can be up to double the prime rates, very limited options of products and rates can vary widely. Lenders have all of the power and control—you are at their mercy. There are fewer regulations with sub-prime loans; therefore, there are more predators looking for opportunities to take advantage of you and those loans often have harsh pre-payment penalties.

Regardless of the loan you choose, fixed-rate or adjustable rate, prime or sub-prime, always have an exit strategy. American homeowners live in their homes an average of eight years, three years for first-time homebuyers. Before purchasing your home, map out how long you plan to live in the house and select your mortgage accordingly. As part of setting your financial goals, answer some key questions for yourself.

- Why this home and why now?
- Is it in an emerging neighborhood?
- Is it a good investment?

- Is it the right size for your family at the time?
- When will it be time to move out, will it be a set dollar amount in profit? An increase in family size? The next career level when it makes sense? A set time period? A lifestyle modification such as finishing a level of education or getting married?
- What do I want to do with my profits? Participate in an investment vehicle, stocks, bonds, or an IRA?? Buying an investment or vacation home? Invest it into the next house? Start a business?

You won't always have solid, firm answers to those questions, but by at least considering them while you are making your decision, it gives you a template to work from and refer back to as part of your overall financial plans and goals.

You are now armed with the tools from my years of experience and millions of dollars in funded mortgage loans. By having this knowledge, you own leverage in any meeting that you have with your loan officer. A good loan officer appreciates an educated client. You are their dream customer. You will know what you want and why you want it. You can talk about your financial goals, your long and short-term strategies, and your plans for this house and your next five houses down the road. Always talk about your goals with a mortgage professional. You want a teammate, not a transaction. You should be able to count on your loan officer as your first source for all major transactions. Your loan officer should have a team of a CPA, financial planner, investment consultant, realtor, attorney, and a banker. If they don't have that team, then you need to find a better mortgage professional. They need you more than you need them. This team is your key to maximizing financial professionals to your benefit.

- What steps are you prepared to take to fulfill your part of the American Dream?
- What does your dream house look like in your mind and how are you going to get started TODAY down the path to homeownership to eventually reach that goal?

NOTES:

Chapter 9:

Taking the Next Steps in Building Wealth

Everything you have read up to this point has been with the sole purpose of preparing you to become wealthy through a solid financial plan. Comedian Chris Rock said the difference between being rich and wealthy is that riches die when you die and wealth lasts for generations. There's a lot of truth in that joke. I want you to strive to be wealthy. There is no magic formula for becoming wealthy; however, there are some time-proven methods that when implemented properly will make a significant positive impact on your family's financial future.

You've just read a chapter on the process of homeownership but how about the value? Did you know that the national average is 8% appreciation per year. Some markets are more, some are less but that's a great return on your investment. Rarely do get-rich-quick deals work out in real estate however so be smart and prudent. Don't just over-buy and hope for the best. Make smart decisions, don't chase a trend without researching it's long term benefits and potential pitfalls. Your house should be an asset as well as a home. Learn how to use the equity as capital for other endeavors.

One secret of the mortgage business is that you can own multiple second homes. As long as a second home is at least 150 miles away from your primary residence and you will use it for up to two consecutive weeks throughout the year, it is considered a second home. You can buy these homes as a true second home, but also use it as an investment. Rent the house for the remainder of the time that you are not living there, but make sure that you plan to occupy it for at least two weeks throughout the year. The major benefit of purchasing a house as a second home are; lower down payment requirements vs. investment property and typically you will be getting an interest rate similar to the rates for a primary residence. Don't commit loan fraud, however, by buying an investment property and trying to call it a second home. Penalties for loan fraud include the mortgage being called due immediately, significant fines and imprisonment. It is not worth it.

You can also purchase investment properties. They can be a source for consistent residual income and, on rare occasions, you can buy low, renovate, and sell months later for a quick profit. There are expenses involved, such as maintenance, property management companies and the risk of un-rented units. Investment properties often require at least a 10% down payment and reserves of your mortgage payment after closing, but consult your mortgage professional for more details.

A potential untapped market is purchasing builder-model homes. Often you can buy at phase one prices, lease it back to the builder, and then sell it at final phase prices for a profit. These deals can be tricky and require a 10% down payment as well, so consult your mortgage professional or builder specialist for more details.

Financial planners and advisors will always tell you to invest in your company's 401(k) plan. According to

Dante McDowell of National Financial Services Group in Atlanta, GA, the primary reason to invest in a 401k is most companies will match up to a certain percentage of what you contribute. You invest your money and the company gives you free money. Not a bad deal at all. Generally speaking, the recommendation is for people to contribute the percentage of up to what the company will match. In other words, if the company offers to match dollar for dollar up to 6%, then you should contribute 6% of your salary and get the full match from the company. Any contributions above that, you are simply deferring paying the taxes and that may not be in your best interest at distribution.

If a person's income is such that maxing out their 401(k) contribution would significantly reduce their overall taxable income or reduce their tax bracket, or if they are in a heavy catch-up mode, shortening the timeframe to retirement, then by all means do so. Otherwise, contribute to get the company's full match and find other alternatives for retirement savings.

Investing in an IRA: McDowell adds, for most folks, Roth IRAs are great vehicles to accumulate retirement funds because 1) all tax funds grow tax-deferred; and 2) all withdrawals are tax-free, because the funds going in have already been taxed. (Some restrictions apply, consult your financial planner for specific advice) Also, funds from Roth IRAs can be accessed to fund education expenses or to purchase your first home tax-free and penalty free, if certain conditions are met, of course. But Roth gives you a lot of flexibility in saving and giving time to grow can be a huge asset during retirement.

Investing in stocks, bonds, money markets, or CDs: Mc Dowell advises that to achieve long-term success and accumulate wealth, one must invest in the stock market. Despite some volatile moments, our stock market produces between 10 and 11% return over time. But that is the key — time. Same with bonds — if given ample time, bonds can produce consistent income and downside protection in a portfolio. Over time, bonds will average between 5 and 6%. In order to achieve maximum results, one must diversify and have a mixture of stocks and bonds that fit their risk tolerance. Timeframes have to be taken into consideration and use of the funds that are being invested.

Money markets are good for safe-keeping. Depending on the bank, money markets can generate interest-income from anywhere from 1%-5%. This is good for short-term investing and emergency funds. However, it is not good for long-term capital appreciation.

Certificates of Deposit (CDs) are good for safe-keeping as well, but do not offer the instant liquidity of money markets. CDs will guarantee a rate of return if the funds stay in the account for a set period. If an investor wants no risk and and is willing to commit those funds for stated period of time, CDs can be good. However, they are not good for long-term growth.

Mc Dowell concludes with a couple of steps for young investors or someone beginning a savings plan.

1) Just get started. Most mutual funds will begin a systematic monthly investment for an investor at $50 a month — some people as little as $25.

2) Invest with a purpose. Ask yourself "what are these funds going to be used for and when do I want to use them?" You may have a 401(k) at work and a Roth IRA for retirement or you may have a money market account for emergency cash reserves. Define what those funds are earmarked for and invest accordingly.

3) ***Stick to your investment plan.*** Understand that things happen and you may have to stop that $50 going into that mutual fund or IRA this month, but as soon as you are able, get back to your plan. Get in the market and stay in the market.

A good resource to research information on investing and other money matters is *MSN Money.* Their articles are usually very informative and you can do research on just about any investment. *Yahoo!* (www.yahoo.com) also has a personal business and finance page dedicated to financial education.

Remember, wealth is built for generations, so why not start immediately for you and for your next generation?

- What steps are you going to take to begin your savings and wealth building plan?
- What are the 3 new ways you will invest in yourself and save money over the next 90 days?

NOTES:

Chapter 10:

Sharing the Knowledge

Now that you've seen the blueprint and understand the importance of credit, homeownership and wealth building principles, make wealth a family principal—something that becomes part of your life and lifestyle. Teach your children about credit as soon as they're able to understand it. When a child is ready for his or her first car, explain all that goes in to making that purchase. Teach them budgeting. Teach them the importance of timely payments and homeownership at a young adult age. Teach them financial goal setting and have them set up achievable mini-goals. Help them achieve their mini-goals along the way to setting and achieving larger goals.

Set their financial footsteps in your footsteps and missteps. Share with your children the family finances—positive and negative. Sit with them when you are doing your monthly budget and bills. Educate them about taxes, mortgages, insurance, and everything that goes in to running the household.

By giving your children the benefit of educating them early, you can ensure their financial future and them continuing the cycle of wealth for future generations in your family.

In addition to this book, I have also prepared the *Control Your Credit Destiny Workbook and Software* to help you achieve your financial goals and fulfill your credit destiny.

In the *Control Your Credit Destiny Workbook and*

Software you will find:

- Estimates vs. Actual Costs worksheet.
- Weekly Spending Tracker worksheet.
- Your Wants vs. Your Needs worksheet.
- Income and Assets worksheet.
- Monthly and Annual Budget.
- Goal-Setting and Tracking worksheet.
- A page for you to do your personal BHAGs.

In addition to the *Control Your Credit Desitiny Workbook and Software*, I also have a *Control Your Credit Destiny Credit Repair Kit* that can help you get back on the path to financial freedom, rebuild a strong credit history, and help you get back on the path to repairing your credit to ensure strong credit and financial future.

These are vital tools to achieving your financial goals and attaining financial freedom and wealth.

Now that you know the secrets of the credit scoring formulas, the Rule of 3—2—1, the secrets of taking power in the homeownership process and some wealth-building strategies, the world is at your fingertips.

Remember, it's never too late to start to establish good credit and wealth building principles. It starts one day, week or month at time.

While credit and personal finance are truly personal things, we all know people who struggle with some of the basics you just read about. Tell them there's a book out there that can help them reach the same place you are going—their own credit destiny.

GLOSSARY OF TERMS

- Adjustable Rate Mortgage (ARM)-A mortgage with a rate that is fixed for a set period of time and will subsequently adjust there after.

- BHAG-Big Hairy Audacious Goal. An acronym often used in corporate America to set a benchmark for achievement.

- Charge Off-A past due account that a company ceases pursuit of payment but remains as an outstanding balance on an individual's credit report.

- Closing costs-Fees paid by the customer to close a mortgage loan. Fees usually include realtor, lender and title company costs as well as profit for all parties.

- Collection-A past due account sold to a third party for them to pursue payment from an individual.

- Collection Agency-A third party that purchases delinquent debts and pursues the individual owing the debt.

- Compounding Interest-A percentage of your savings that a financial institution pays you for keeping your money in their institution.

- Consumer Credit Counseling Services (CCCS)-A non profit agency that assists in managing personal consumer debt and attempts to settle lower payments or settlement amounts.

- Consumer Debt-The amount that individuals owe to banks or financial institutions used to purchase items via a loan or credit card.

- Credit Score-A measure of credit worthiness determined by various factors. Banks and financial institutions use the credit scores provided to them by credit reporting bureaus Equifax, Experian and Trans Union to help determine approval and interest rates for financing.

- Debt balance-The amount of an installment or revolving loan that is currently unpaid.

- Delinquent Payments-Payments submitted 30 days or more after the due date on a given account.

- Discharged Bankruptcy-After a bankruptcy filing when the individual complies with the court's directives for fulfilling their debts.

- Dismissed Bankruptcy-After a bankruptcy filing when the individual does not comply with the court's directives for fulfilling their debts.

- Equity-The amount of value your house has that is not tied to your mortgage balance. (Example: Home's value is $250,000 and mortgage balance is $200,000. Equity value is $50,000.)

- Fannie Mae/Freddie Mac-Agencies that purchase most 'prime' or conventional mortgages originated.

- Federal Housing Administration (FHA)-The largest mortgage insurer in the world, insures mortgages originated under its programs. Typically allows higher loans to values and lower credit scores than conventional (Fannie Mae/Freddie Mac) loans.

- Finance Company Cards-Cards applied for and granted for purchase at a specific store (Example: Best Buy, Rooms To Go, etc.) that are backed by an independent financial institution.

- Fixed Rate Mortgage-A mortgage with a rate

that is fixed for the term of the loan.

- Foreclosure-Repossession of real estate by the lending institution for lack of payment.

- Foreclosure Buy-out/Pre Foreclosure- An individual purchasing a property that is in foreclosure proceedings before the bank takes possession.

- Home Equity Line of Credit (HELOC)-A loan based upon the amount of equity you have in your home. A HELOC usually allows you to treat it as a revolving account but the credit scoring models read it as an installment account when over $25,000.

- Home Equity Loan-A loan based on your equity but is cannot be re-utilized once paid down or off.

- Individual Retirement Account (IRA)- Savings accounts that usually are tax deferred until retirement with a penalty for early withdrawal.

- Installment Accounts-Credit accounts with a set loan amount that when paid down cannot be utilized again. (Examples: Mortgage, Automobile loan, personal unsecured loans.)

- Judgment-A legal decision obligating one party to pay another which is recorded in court records.

- Lien-A financial amount levied against a party that attaches to real estate or other property the individual owns until it is paid or settled.

- Loan to Value-The amount of a mortgage balance in relation to the value of the property. (Example: $200,000 mortgage balance on a home valued at $250,000 is an 80% loan to value or LTV.)

- New Construction-Homes newly constructed that have never been lived in or owned before.

- Pay Option ARM-Adjustable rate mortgage popularized in the early 2000's that offers the borrower multiple payment options and interest rates each month for their mortgage payment.

- Piggyback Loan-A first and second mortgage typically used to avoid PMI by putting 80% or less on the first mortgage and the balance on the second mortgage.

- Pre-payment penalty-A penalty levied by a loan servicer for paying off a mortgage before a pre-determined period of time. Usually equal to 6 months worth of mortgage interest.

- Private Mortgage Insurance (PMI)-Insurance a mortgage borrower pays for that insures the lender if there is less than 20% equity in the property.

- Reserves-Savings equivalent to a monthly payment of a mortgage, auto loan, etc.

- Revolving Accounts-Credit accounts with a set high credit amount with the ability to pay down and re-utilize the credit line. (Examples: Credit cards, small personal equity loans)

- Secured Loan-A loan that is placed on a piece of real estate as collateral for repayment of the loan.

- Sub-Prime loans-Mortgages typically offered to customers with poor credit and/or unverifiable income. These mortgages usually are have a higher interest rate, more loan fees and pre-payment penalties.

- Unsecured Loan-A loan that has no real estate collateral involved.